Minute Motivators for Teachers

Stan Toler

RIVER
OAK
PUBLISHING

Tulsa, Oklahoma

06 05 04 03 02   10 9 8 7 6 5 4 3 2 1

Minute Motivators for Teachers
ISBN 1-58919-984-7
Copyright © 2002 by Stan Toler

Published by RiverOak Publishing
P.O. Box 70013
Tulsa, Oklahoma 74170-0143

Introduction

Teachers don't need any more apples.

They need a friend and some friendly advice—advice from someone who appreciates who they are and not just what they do. This book isn't about final answers. Rather, it's about searching for excellence—a search that ends up enhancing the self as well as the student.

Written from the "homeroom" of my heart, Minute Motivators for Teachers is offered to share dynamic truths with professionals who have illuminated the world with such tools as an overhead projector, a bulletin board, and an encouraging word.

Stan Toler

Teach to influence lives.

"As speakers, we aren't the wings. We are the wind beneath the wings."

—Rosanne Emmerich

INFLUENCE

If you were to name the great teachers of all time, what qualities of theirs would stand out? You would probably conclude that they didn't just teach others; they influenced them. Their lives, as well as their teachings, still impact individuals and societies. What they taught was simply an extension of who they were. They influenced others because of their character.

Devotion, commitment, compassion, diligence —these qualities were undoubtedly the disciplines of their lives, the dynamic that made them Hall of Fame teachers. They were more than purveyors of facts or figures. They modeled a value system that caused others to remember them for what they stood for as well as what they taught.

Make it your goal to affect not only the minds of your students but their lives as well. Influence them. Lead them. Let your personal disciplines be a classroom where your students will learn how to live, and not just how to spell or count. If that's your goal, your work will go on long after you're gone.

Great teachers don't produce a product; they produce an effect.

Prepare
to excel.

"He who prepares well,

teaches well."

—Stan Toler

PREPARATION

Where do you want to be professionally in the next five years? What will it take to get there? Preparation. It takes preparation! Excellence isn't accidental. It comes by applying yourself to a training regimen. Olympians don't accidentally become great athletes. Granted, some of their skills are innate. Some are born with the propensity for athletic greatness. But for the most part, athletic ability is the result of disciplined practice. The same principle applies to teaching greatness. What kind of preparation will you need to make?

First, learn from those who've gone before you. In any field of endeavor, the success of others is a great source of instruction. What successful methods and practices can be applied to your own profession?

Second, constantly develop your skills. Plan a "PIT" Stop (Personal Improvement Time). Just as a race-car driver plans pit stops for refueling, refreshments, and mechanical adjustments, there are times when you'll need to stop what you are doing and use the down time for professional refueling, refreshing, and adjustment.

Before you prepare a lesson plan, you must first prepare yourself.

Value the potential of each student.

"Everyone is to be valued and made to feel worthwhile."

—Mary Vaughn

POTENTIAL

A gardener doesn't raise a crop of roses. He cultivates the flowers one bloom at a time. It's the same with a teacher. Never make it your goal to teach one hundred students; rather, make it your goal to teach one. Learn to see the value of the individual. Look for each student's personal potential.

Each student represents an opportunity to change the world. The principles you share with one person may potentially influence the lives of countless others. But that influence will not be realized without personal attention to the one. A personal word, an encouraging note, a personal concern—it takes very little to make a great impact.

Throughout the Bible, we see Jesus picking out solitary people in the midst of a crowd and personally ministering to them. Everyone was important to Him—one at a time. No one was a throwaway. Each had a unique potential.

So focus on a single rose rather than on a rosebush. Potential greatness sits before you—no matter how many thorns are showing!

Look for the future in every student.

Focus on encouragement.

"We should be in the business of building people up. There's too many people in the demolition business today."

—Norman Vincent Peale

ENCOURAGEMENT

Some of your students will probably have taken a beating even before they got to school. Maybe they haven't been physically beaten, but some have been psychologically beaten. Perhaps discouraging words have been used as sticks and stones, and their potential has been bruised and battered by the selfish attitudes and actions of others.

These students are scattered throughout your classroom. Perhaps a younger child has come from a desperate home. Maybe there's an older student who is dealing with the fear of failure, or a teenager who is facing tremendous pressure from a peer. Today is your opportunity to stop the abuse—if only for a few hours.

Your word may be the only encouraging word they will hear today. Your smile may be their only smile. Your praise may be their only praise.

God has given you the singular opportunity to reverse the emotional direction of your students. You have the power to lift a countenance, the chance to bring emotional life to the wounded, the opportunity to raise a sprig of hope in a forest of discouragement.

Good words have power to build the spirit. Use them.

Rely on your training.

"I have never let my
schooling get in the
way of my education."

—Mark Twain

CONFIDENCE

Y ou can do this. Sure, there will be challenges. You'll face questions that you can't answer. You'll meet students who are unmotivated and unruly. You'll deal with administrators who don't support your ideas. But you can handle it. You've been through years of training to reach this point. Now it's time to test that training.

You've learned the skills necessary for this task, and you've practiced those skills under the watchful eyes of a supervising teacher. You've studied the advice of wise educators. Now, you are an extension of their proven theories. Trust them, even as you trust yourself.

You're not alone. You have a support system. Your professors had enough confidence in your ability to give you that passing grade. Your colleagues are by your side. They are confident of the system that brought you to this day.

Also, you're doing the right thing. You are spending your life enriching the lives of others, and you can't go wrong by doing right.

"C" is more than a passing grade as long as it stands for "confidence!"

Cultivate a good relationship with students.

"So long as we love we serve.
No man is useless
while he is a friend."

—Robert Louis Stevenson

RELATIONSHIP

The old model portrayed the teacher as an expert. The students knew nothing; the teacher knew everything. Students were to sit in rapt attention while the teacher poured forth figures and philosophies. Times have changed. This is the interactive age. Monologue has been replaced with dialogue. Your student looks for a mentor, not a guru. He or she looks for a friend, not a fact-giver. Learning happens best where there's trust, and trust comes from relationship.

Spend time building bridges of communication to your students. Certainly, some professional boundaries must be in place. But learning how to speak "to" students is better than continuing to speak "at" them.

Get to know them. What are their dreams? What motivates them? How can you ring their "interest bell"? Let them get to know you. Transparency is not a disease. It's a dynamic—a dynamic that will help you transfer knowledge effectively and personally.

Long after the lesson has been forgotten, the personality of the teacher will be remembered. When you communicate on a personal level, knowledge has a friendly face.

Learn the value of a great story.

"Word pictures create power

in communication."

—Stan Toler

STORYTELLING

Stories have power. The greatest books in our literature are stories. In movie-making, a captivating story will mean the difference between box office success or box office failure. Even the best movie wardrobe, sound, or effects are wasted if there isn't a good story line. Everyone loves a well-told tale. Use the power of a story in your teaching. Stories are effective word-paintings that stir the imaginations of your students and provide a "branch" where you can hang a fact or figure.

Collect and file stories that illustrate the truths you teach. Magazines, newspaper articles, and the news or documentaries are veritable gold mines for stories that will illustrate your lessons. Drop them into lesson plans. Give them as reading assignments. Use good stories creatively. Tell them drama-tically—leading your audience to the punch line, not pushing them toward it.

You have a point to make, so make it pointedly! Let the fable, tale, or parable make your point for you. A little pizzazz will turn a boring presentation into a memorable one.

Harness the power of a story.

Look like you're having fun!

"A smile is worth a million dollars, but it doesn't cost a cent."

—Talmadge Johnson

ENTHUSIASM

Ask a fifth-grader what he thinks of school and most likely he'll answer, "It's boring." Never let that be true of your teaching. Enthusiasm is one of the great keys to effective communication. As long as you read with some enthusiasm, you could read the pages of a telephone directory out loud and keep someone's attention!

Enthusiasm begins at home. It's a state of mind. Look forward to your work each day. Think about the positives. You'll have plenty of time to encounter a negative or two! Use your driving time to "switch gears." Play a motivational or humorous CD or tape instead of listening to bad news or traffic-jam reports. (Those traffic jams will wait for you.) Capture the moment and let your mind be taken captive by positive thoughts.

Enthusiasm also begins with the lesson plan. "How can I put a little excitement into this lesson?" "What can I do or say to give these important facts a life of their own?"

Your students won't take delight in learning until you take delight in teaching.

Master the pregnant pause.

"The secret of being a bore
is to tell everything."

—Voltaire

TIMING

Great comedians have one thing in common: great timing. Timing adds punch to the delivery of a joke—or just about anything. Some of the classic monologues include that moment when the comedian stops his or her delivery and just gives a look. Done skillfully, even the pause or look elicits howling laughter or applause.

For a teacher, great timing means knowing when to speak and when to be silent. You probably won't hear a lot of applause in the classroom, but a well-timed "stop" can be one of the most effective tools in your "teaching kit." It can force the student to think. It can emphasize the value of what you've just said. It also can focus attention on what you say next.

Great teachers are great communicators. They "go to school" on the styles and skills of other speakers. They study good communication methodology. Then they practice.

Knowing when to speak is good. Knowing when to be silent is even better. Master the pause. It will double the value of your words.

Acknowledge your mistakes.

"The man who is incapable
of making a mistake is
incapable of anything."

—Abraham Lincoln

HONESTY

It's not a matter of if, but when. Sooner of later, it will happen. You will make a mistake. You'll give the wrong information in response to a question. You'll assign homework without proper preparation. You'll have to reverse a decision you've made. That's okay. Everybody makes mistakes, and nobody minds it—as long as you admit it, that is.

Honesty really is the best policy. Honesty is a character quality, an important part of anyone's value system. But it's especially important to teachers, whose very lives should model those values. Honesty is a great validation, giving credence to other teachings. Honesty is also a great communication bridge. Teachers whose lives are open and honest before their students have a greater opportunity to communicate with them.

Go ahead and admit that you are human. Your students already know it, and the fact that you are willing to be transparent to them will actually work in your favor.

When you're quick to admit error and are willing to extend an apology, your students will actually give you a better grade.

Build students through verbal praise.

"There is no greater burden
than human potential."

—Charlie Brown

PRAISE

Often, the president of the United States will make a congratulatory phone call to give a word of praise to someone who has made a noteworthy achievement. How would you feel if you received such a call? Being singled out for that kind of attention would make you feel pretty good, wouldn't it?

Your personal attention can have a similarly positive effect on your students. A simple word of encouragement could be just the thing to propel a student to even greater achievement. Praise students when they do something right. Call them by name and say, "Great job!" Look for opportunities to affirm their hard work. Make a public announcement. Honor them by honoring their accomplishments.

When you praise a student, you are building his or her self-esteem. You are affirming the student's individual worth. When you praise a student, you are acknowledging that he or she is a person and not just an ID number. You are also helping the student realize a step of maturity.

Praise is the fuel that powers mastery.

Become a lifelong learner.

"The person who graduates today and stops learning tomorrow is uneducated the day after."

—Loren Gresham

CURIOSITY

In order to keep teaching, you must keep learning. The very nature of your profession demands a cutting-edge curiosity. In a world where new theories are as frequent as the sunrise, yesterday's facts need to be freshened up. By becoming a lifelong learner, you'll always be a step ahead of your colleagues—or at least in step with them.

Never lose your sense of curiosity. Let it drive you to new discoveries about your subject. What's your specialty? What's new in that area? Are you curious about other subjects? Do you have a "broadband" knowledge or do you have "single line" knowledge? What is your "current events quotient"? A good mix of history and current events will give you a greater context in which to communicate with your students.

And speaking of students, are you curious about them? How do they differ from last year's class? What drives them? Your curiosity about their culture will help you understand them and subsequently reach them.

Because you are a teacher, you must also be a lifelong student.

Invest your life in the student.

"Small deeds done are better than great deeds planned."

—Peter Marshall

GIVING

As a teacher, you not only give lessons to your students; you give your very life. Every day, in little pieces of time, energy, or emotion, you give a part of yourself. You also give them the best part of your day, the best days of your week, and the best years of your life.

But is it really a gift? Isn't it rather one of the wisest investments you will ever make? You exchange your skill for their understanding. And most often, that understanding will be used for the betterment of society. You exchange your devotion for their admiration. And most often, that admiration will be used as a model for building personal character.

Often, teaching seems to be so unidirectional. In actuality, it is an exciting cycle of investment and rewards. What you give now will be realized in some reciprocal action. You may not be around when it happens, but eventually your investment will pay off.

You're not just a teacher. You are an investor—bartering your time and effort for the wealth that cannot be counted.

Determine to love the unlovable.

"Nothing you do for children is ever wasted."

—Garrison Keillor

LOVE

There's one in every class: that one student who tries your patience, wears on your nerves, and makes you wonder why you ever became a teacher. Unteachable, unbearable, unlovable—those are the words that will run through your mind. Think again. It really is worth the time to consider the cause behind that child's effect. That unruly student may be a "prisoner of war." You don't know the raging wars that he or she may be facing—a tortured home life, emotional pain, or physical illness.

Unlovely? Perhaps. Unlovable? Never. That "problem child" is a child of God, the focus of His best affection. According to the Bible, He cared enough to sacrifice His own Son for the spiritual welfare of that one child.

Pause for a moment and pray for an infusion of compassion. It could just be that the "unlovable" is looking for love—and you just might be the source! At least in your heart, you can give that unruly student a new status: loved, understood, and worthy of honor.

For Heaven's sake, don't give up on that child.

Teach the joy of discovery.

"The mediocre teacher tells, the good teacher explains. The superior teacher demonstrates. The great teacher inspires."

—William Arthur Ward

SERENDIPITY

Putting several students in the same room and equipping them with exciting information is like dropping a match into a gas tank. When the two get together, something is bound to happen! There is a glorious moment in the learning process when the "lights come on." It's the moment when ideas dawn, when something just "clicks" in the learner's brain. That's the moment of discovery, and nothing compares to it!

Of course you know that the experience isn't entirely accidental. There's planning involved. There's a blueprint drawn first in your imagination that will lead your students toward completion. There's creativity involved. There's a searching for unique ways to present classic principles. There's tenacity. There's a commitment in your heart not to give up until the light has dawned and the discovery has been joyfully made.

Let it be your daily goal to lead your students to experience that joy, to lead them toward a discovery. Don't tell them; draw them. Let them experience the excitement of an "Aha!" moment. Learning is a joy. Let your students know it.

Stay informed.

"Sixty years ago, I knew
everything; now I know
nothing; education is a
progressive discovery of
our own ignorance."

—Will Durant

INFORMATION

We live in an information age, and the information changes almost daily. Organizations change. Facts change. Discoveries are made. Methods become out-moded. What was true a day ago may be untrue today or—worse yet—irrelevant. The teacher is the student's guide through the information jungle. It's the teacher's job to know not only what is true, but also what matters.

That means keeping up on current events. It means reading periodicals, listening to the news, asking questions, and doing research. Our world is "wired" for knowledge—from the living room to the library. In most cases, information is only a mouse click away. World events are no longer "over there." The world has come to us.

Staying informed also means being knowledgeable of current methods of communication. Seminars, either on-line or on-site, are available to keep your professional skills fine-tuned. Keep up with trade journals. Take a refresher class. Join a study group. Have someone evaluate your presentations. Make the commitment to do whatever it takes to stay on the cutting edge.

Life is an information superhighway. Don't miss the bus!

Teach within the student's context.

"Education is how kids
learn stuff!"

—Dennis the Menace

CONTEXT

There's a reason why we don't teach algebra to first-graders. They have to learn arithmetic first. Advanced skills can be acquired only after a foundation is laid. Similarly, visual aids are of no value to a sight-impaired student. What good is a video if you can't see it? Every student lives in a unique world. The way in which he or she approaches a subject will be colored by prior learning, economics, physical and mental aptitude, geography, nationality, family of origin, and many more influences.

This principle may seem simple in theory, but how about the practice? Learning how to present "user-friendly" truths takes discipline. Find out where your students are. How will you link what they "need to understand" with what they already understand? It's entirely possible to make our school buildings accessible and yet make our teachings inaccessible. Barriers to real learning must be removed. Creative methods must be employed. When you build the learning house in familiar surroundings, the student will be less likely to get lost on the journey.

Remember that a text without context is merely a pretext.

Share daily points of light.

"A human being is not, in any proper sense, a human being until he is educated."

—Horace Mann

LEADERSHIP

The person who aims for nothing will hit it every time. A good teacher gives students something to shoot for. Good teachers have "inner leaders." They are not content to force-feed theories and statistics and are challenged by the thought of leading students to a point of personal discovery.

Of course, part of the teaching process is creating the desire for learning. Motivate your students with "points of light." Create the model before their very eyes. Lift up achievements for them to emulate. Invite local "heroes" to your classroom—former students who have achieved success. Let them see for themselves the effects of learning, application, and diligence.

Teach your students to set personal standards of excellence. Point them toward goals that they can reach, and give them incentives for achieving their objectives.

Make it personal. Show them how your subject will help them outside the classroom. Use current people and events as living lessons. Let them see greatness, and they will be more likely to aim for it.

Give your students a goal worth the getting, and they'll reach it every time.

Never put a student down.

"Education makes people easy to lead, but difficult to drive; easy to govern, but impossible to enslave."

—Lord Brousham

PATIENCE

If you're any good as a teacher, your students will experience frustration. That's because you'll be stretching them. You'll be leading them to discovery, to change. Like a snake shedding its skin, sometimes they'll be uncomfortable as they grow. That discomfort may manifest itself in unpleasant ways. They may even lash out at you. But don't lash back. They may act out with disruptive behavior. Be firm, but be gentle.

Patience really is a virtue. Built into your character system, it is a shining example of maturity. Remember, you are teaching with your life as well as your textbook. You may need to view patience as a skill that needs improvement, along with your other teaching methods. Relaxation, spiritual meditation, and exercise are techniques that can be employed to help you be more patient. Students need a "time out" to focus on their behavior once in a while. Maybe teachers need a time out as well. Choose your words and actions carefully. In some regards, they will last forever.

Patience is learned one student at a time!

Practice team-building.

"Coming together is a
beginning; keeping
together is progress;
working together is success."

—Henry Ford

TEAMWORK

The best way to limit your accomplishments is to try doing everything yourself. But when you work with others, you multiply your effectiveness. You probably learned the adage as a child: "Many hands make light work." It's true. More often, "lone rangers" tire before they triumph. It's better to build your students into a team and work with them than to work for them. You'll not only alleviate some stress, you'll provide others with an opportunity to learn and serve as well.

You'll soon see yourself as a player-coach who is more concerned about seeing a team win than seeing an individual star. Team-building is an art. It takes heaps of encouragement, tons of praise, and a truckload of patience. It also takes careful delegation and follow-up. But the results are worth it.

Collaborate with your peers. Harness their energy; share your ideas. Divide the labor; don't reinvent the wheel. Train your students to work together, and you'll give them a life-direction that they will never regret.

A team of two will accomplish three times more than two individuals.

Ask God to make you an effective communicator.

"Do not conform any longer to the pattern of this world, but be transformed by the renewing of your mind. Then you will be able to test and approve what God's will is—his good, pleasing and perfect will."

—Romans 12:2

FAITH

Many great communicators were terrible speakers. Moses comes to mind. When asked to lead the children of Israel, the Old Testament standout argued that he wasn't an eloquent speaker. But his words not only influenced the people of Bible times; they have influenced people throughout time. What was the difference? He didn't take a speech class. He didn't study self-improvement tapes or join a Toastmasters club. There's nothing wrong with any of those improvement techniques, but they're not the reason Moses became a great communicator and leader.

Moses excelled because he put his faith in God's plan, and God gave him a spokesman to take up the communication slack. Faith always makes the difference. Do you believe that you can motivate a child? You can. Do you have faith that you can be an effective teacher? You can be. No, you may not have all the answers or all the skills. That's okay. Ask God to make you effective in your work.

First, believe that God will help you reach your audience. Then, go ahead and speak up!

Don't expect immediate results.

"School is a building that
has four walls—with
tomorrow inside."

—Lon Walters

EXPECTATION

We're used to instant results. Computer technology has led us to believe that anything requiring more than a few seconds is slow. But good things take time. It takes fifty years or so to grow a good tree, tall and strong. Building fine furniture requires a craftsman's skill; that takes time. And forming a mature mind takes time too. You've learned not to judge a class by their first day's behavior. You've also learned not to judge a student by the results of that first pop quiz.

Be patient with yourself as well. Don't judge your work by one day's results. Take a longer view. Make your investment of time, energy, and skill now, and then learn to expect a return—even if it takes a while. Excellence is a process, not an event.

Expect the same for your students. Look for growth over a month, a year, or a lifetime. Allow time for maturity. Let the seeds of knowledge grow into wisdom and respect into character. Be patient. The most important things take time.

Always tell the truth.

"Do the right thing. It will
please some people and
astonish others."

—Mark Twain

INTEGRITY

Trust is the foundation of any relationship. It's the glue that binds people together. Without trust, there is no hope of a long-term friendship or association. The relationship between teacher and student is no different. If your students trust you, they will trust what you say.

Build that trust by being honest—by always telling the truth. When you don't know, say so. When you're wrong, admit it. Avoid "white lies," "half truths," and rationalizations. They seem harmless, but they destroy the precious trust that a student places in a teacher.

Be known by your integrity. Let it be said of you that you are as good as your word. No, you can't keep all of your promises. Circumstances and time will prevent that. But you can try. You can make a personal pledge to do what you say, if at all possible. That goes for keeping a confidence as well. The trust given to you by your associates has great value. Words spoken in confidence are confidential—period.

Tell the truth—all the time—and you'll teach more than one lesson in your classroom.

Be hopeful.

"Things never go so well that
one should have no fear nor
so ill that one should
have no hope."

—Danish Proverb

OPTIMISM

Despair is the enemy of progress. When u spirit of pessimism winds its way into a corporation, community, or classroom, the results are demoralizing and defeating. When hope is lost, all is lost. Hope is the foundation of any success.

When you despair of making a difference in your classroom, you won't. If you allow yourself to become discouraged, your students will become discouraged too. But, like despair, hope is infectious. A spirit of optimism can change any environment—especially the classroom. And it all begins with you! You're the source. Your hopefulness breeds hope. Your optimistic spirit puts the "can do" into the people and projects that surround you on a daily basis.

When you believe that the student can learn, he or she will probably believe it as well. When you believe that you are teaching truths that can revolutionize individuals and communities, your students will believe it too.

Optimism pays fantastic dividends—for you as well as for your students. Believe that you can change the world. You are doing it every day.

Get your time under control.

"I wasted time; now time doth waste me."

—William Shakespeare

DISCIPLINE

Have you ever felt short of time? Actually, time is the only thing everyone has in common. Everyone has the same supply of hours and minutes with which to face the day. How that "currency" of time is spent often means the difference between success and failure. Those who have learned to control time—to discipline it—are those who avoid the stress of having to do things at the last minute and the authority that the urgent has over them.

Most of us don't need more time; we need to use our time better. Discipline is a critical skill for any teacher. Capture your loose minutes, and you will bring your hours under control. Schedule your time. Give yourself a time parameter and work within that allotted time. Look for other time-wasters. For example, organize the space where you study and teach to make your movements more efficient. Never do anything twice; do it right the first time.

Bring yourself under control, and your classroom will follow.

Be prepared.

"Plans are nothing.
Planning is everything."

—Dwight D. Eisenhower

PREPARATION

The only thing more painful than presenting a disorganized lesson is enduring one. If the teacher isn't prepared, the entire class suffers—student by student. But the toll it takes on the class is minimal compared to the toll it takes on you. Lack of preparation will raise your stress level to record-breaking heights. That's why it's to your advantage to prepare yourself now, rather than suffering the palm-sweating later on.

Take some stress out of your day by planning it ahead of time. Begin early in the day. First, prepare your mind. Start the day with some positive thinking. "This will be a good day!" "I can make it happen today!"

Second, prepare your heart. Read from the most positive book on the shelf—your Bible. Let God's powerful, written Word encourage you and direct your day.

Third, prepare your body. Get your heart going with some good exercises.

Fourth, prepare professionally. Create a design for your term and your week, as well as your day. Make a schedule, and stick to it.

A day is a terrible thing to waste.

Be yourself.

"What the teacher is,
is more important that
what one teaches."

—Karl Menninger

AUTHENTICITY

A good teacher communicates content. A great teacher communicates character. Your students will learn as much about you as they learn from you—maybe more! How do you rise to that challenge? Be yourself. If you are honest, they'll learn honesty. If you're humble, they'll learn humility. If you are courageous, they'll learn courage. If you're kind, they'll learn kindness.

Even before you say, "Good morning," you will be teaching. Your lessons won't just be displayed on an erasable board, an overhead, or a video; they'll be displayed in your life as well. Some of the most important lessons you will ever teach will be taught by your own classroom behavior.

Be yourself, and the lesson will be a good one. If you try to be something—or someone—you're not, the lesson will have a negative effect. Your students may not know much about history, geography, or social studies as yet, but they already know human behavior.

So drop the mask and smile your way into someone's heart. Your students will give you an "A" for authentic.

Be resourceful.

"Imagination is the
beginning of creation."

—George Bernard Shaw

RESOURCEFULNESS

The fact is, nobody has all the time, money, stuff, or resources they need. Everyone feels overworked, underfunded, and short-staffed. No matter what your profession, there are times when there is more responsibility than resource. To succeed, you must learn to make the most of what you have. That means being resourceful.

Recycle old ideas and used materials. Maintain a network of associates who have either retired or have been reassigned. They probably have a veritable storehouse of good materials that can be borrowed, begged, or bought.

Need a helping hand? Borrow some help from coworkers, and then loan yourself in return. Skills and experience can be bartered in an interesting display of cooperative effort.

Pinch every penny in your budget until it cries for help. Double up. Carry over. Do it again. Recycle. Reach down into the recesses of your creative spirit and do what you need to do with what you have to work with.

Can you think of fifteen uses for a toothpick? Then you just might be a teacher!

Be accountable.

"Few men have virtue to
withstand the highest bidder."

—George Washington

ACCOUNTABILITY

Accountability isn't a one-way street. Your students are accountable to you. You must be accountable to others. Your credibility depends upon it. Neither your time nor your talent are solely yours. You will be amenable to someone your entire professional career. Of course, that's not a new idea. You knew that even while the ink on your teaching certificate was drying.

Accountability is a progressive behavior. You're not accountable once; you're accountable always. As long as your name is on the paycheck from that corporation, as long as there are students awaiting your arrival in the classroom, you have an ongoing responsibility to give an account of your time, your professional skills, and your personal behavior.

Accountability is a daily habit. When you have reports due to your superiors, make them timely. When you have given your word to your students, keep it. Handle your money with integrity. Be honest in all of your dealings. A teacher's major asset is trust. When others believe what you say, you can be effective. When they don't, you will fail. Protect that trust by making yourself accountable.

Be available.

"The most valuable gift you
can give is time."

—Steve Weber

AVAILABILITY

Teaching isn't a job; it's a profession. People don't teach for a living; they are teachers. Forget the nine-to-five schedule; it doesn't exist. The most important moments in teaching may come outside the structured class time. The question after class, the early morning "bull session," the phone call at home—these are opportunities to do what you do best—teach.

But those things can't happen if you're not available. Learning happens best when it relates to life. That's why those life moments are so important. A whole semester's content about sociology may be forgotten, but that class trip to an ethnic neighborhood in the inner city will probably remain in the minds of your students forever.

You don't have to be a buddy, but you can be a friend. Your speech, mannerisms, or body language can convey that openness to friendship. Certainly you must have an accessibility policy that is fair and reasonable, but those two or three extra minutes after the class session might just be filled with more personal influence than two or three years of structured classroom time.

Be willing to say "I don't know."

"An honest man is the noblest work of God."

—Alexander Pope

CANDOR

Relax. You're not expected to know everything. Your students recognize the difference between being unprepared and simply being human. There's never a penalty for honestly admitting what everybody else already knows: There are some questions you just can't answer. Pretending to know something you don't or denying your ignorance on a subject will harm your credibility.

When you don't know the answer, say that. Your students want the truth—and they want you to be truthful. They live in a world of hype, failed promises, and double-talk. How refreshing it would be for them to have a totally open and honest educational experience. Most will see around that clever turn of a word or phrase. And they understand what it is to have questions—sometimes painfully so.

Teach your students how to live as well as how to learn. Let them know that some of life's problems don't have a solution. They will forever appreciate your honesty, and you will feel so much better about yourself.

Here are the words that lead to a journey of discovery: "I don't know; let's find out."

Expect the unexpected.

"Poise is the ability to be at ease inconspicuously."

—Ann Landers

POISE

Uneventful days can take a sudden twist. You probably learned that as early as your first day of student teaching. Fistfights, fevers, flying objects—you'll see them all sooner or later. You can't anticipate every situation, but you can learn to respond with poise.

Poise starts in your mind. It begins with the realization that you have what it takes to stop the momentary madness (whether you do or not). Inner resolve has a way of surfacing in your outward expressions.

Poise also manifests itself in preparedness. You have a plan B. You have already anticipated that dangerous diversion. You are ready to face the lions with either a chair and whip or a doggie biscuit. You're ready to regain control of the momentary uprising.

Go ahead and expect that your day won't go exactly as planned, and you'll never be disappointed. Actually, you can view classroom interruptions as teaching events. A good teacher can develop a teaching point out of nearly anything. And nearly anything is what you can expect!

Never label students.

"When you say a situation or
a person is hopeless, you are
slamming the door in
the face of God."

—Charles Allen

ACCEPTANCE

Every teacher is a prophet. And what you foretell about a student is likely to come true. Label a student as ignorant, and he will be. Call her a troublemaker, and she won't disappoint you. What you say, either out loud or by your expression, is probably what you will get. Sow the positive, and you'll reap great dividends. Sow the negative, and you'll get what you expect.

Keep an open mind about your students. Accept them as they are, and appreciate them for what they can be. Recognize that an active child isn't necessarily hyperactive. Remember that a student who must work harder at mastery isn't necessarily a slow learner. There is a hidden well of greatness in almost everyone. For example, Einstein failed algebra, but that certainly didn't mean he was a failure.

When you learn how to work with the inner obstacles some students bring to class, you will help your students deal with and overcome them. Your acceptance may be the very thing that propels them to greatness.

Don't put a label on your students. Labels stick.

Respond rather than react.

"Make no little plans; they have no magic to stir men's blood."

—Daniel Burnham

FORESIGHT

Fire drills are a good thing. They enable you to respond with a plan rather than react to an emergency. Anger, embarrassment, and fear—these are reactions. Clarity, decisiveness, and action—these are responses. There's a difference. When you react, you're out of control. When you respond, you exercise control.

Disruptive behavior, passive aggression, abusive language—these are the "emergencies" that you can expect in a classroom. Most often they are symptomatic of a greater problem that the student is dealing with personally. At other times, the student is merely reflecting the behavior he or she has witnessed at home.

How will you face those emergencies? Will you respond, or will you react? If you react, you may heighten the disruption. If you learn to respond, you may quell the disturbance. Think about your strategy. Go through the drills in your mind. "If action A happens, then response A will be employed." Prepare your mind to control your actions. Bring the situation under control by, first, getting yourself under control.

Plan for your own emergencies, and when they happen, you'll respond accordingly.

Tune in to your students' creativity.

"If we love people, we
will see them as God
intends them to be."

—Florence Littauer

OBSERVATION

Every student is gifted in some way. Thinkers, dreamers, planners, motivators, creators, doers—you'll see them all. Every morning, you face a roomful of raw material. You will mine it, refine it, and send it out in the form of talented students with hearts and minds to change their world. Gifts and the gifted must be handled with care. Dealt with carelessly, they may be broken. Dealt with carefully, they are enhanced.

Observe your students. Find out what intrigues them, what inspires them, what makes them tick. Then play to their strengths—and challenge their weaknesses. Potential greatness sits before you with their morning stares and their afternoon yawns. Yours is the task of lighting the fire in them.

Let the actors act; they'll inspire others. Let the dreamers dream; they'll discover a different path. Give the creators some "clay"; you'll be amazed at what they produce. The difference between their mediocrity and their mark of excellence may very well be the encouragement you give them on a daily basis.

Find the greatness and release it.

Celebrate student achievement.

"Whatever a man can conceive
and believe, he can achieve."

—Napoleon Hill

CELEBRATION

Learning is hard work. Creativity burns energy. Discovery usually comes after frustration, trial, and error. That's work! When your students accomplish something, celebrate the achievement. Affirm their efforts, and it will drive them to even greater achievements. Ignore them, and you'll magnify the mediocre.

If your students achieve, let them know you observed it. Just the fact that they caught your attention will often be a source of great motivation. All of us like a nod, a thumbs-up, or a good word.

Take an extra step. Plan a celebration. Find ways to honor what they've done. Is it worth a party—complete with refreshments, banners, and awards? More than likely. The same joy that you experience when that special birthday or anniversary celebration takes place is the joy that will give significance to honored students.

Of course, honors should be evenly distributed. They come in all shapes and sizes to honor various levels of achievement. But they work. They make very human people feel good about their extraordinary efforts.

The moment is worth the medal!

Discover your students' hobbies.

"A hobby is something
you go wild about to
keep from going crazy."

—Jack Benny

INVESTIGATION

Most students don't live for the classroom; they live in spite of it! Usually, the things that interest them most happen outside the four walls of the school building and outside your contact with them. Their lives are often filled with special interests that you aren't even aware of. Whether it's sports, music, pets, clubs, or hobbies, there will be something that will capture the extra-curricular imagination of each student. Find out what that is, and use it as a building block to develop a learning relationship with your students.

A little investigation is in order. Why? Because your students' education depends on it. You can use their natural interests as links to other interests. Learn what they do at home, after school, on weekends. Then, use that knowledge to influence your teaching methods.

Learning isn't a one-way street with a dead end. It's an exciting superhighway, with untold exit and entrance ramps. Discovering those exits and entrances can mean the difference between learning and laboring. Draw parallels between the students' hobbies and your subject. Only then will the "light" shine.

Coach students to develop good study patterns.

"Do your best to present
yourself to God as one
approved, a workman
who does not need to be
ashamed and who correctly
handles the word of truth."

—2 Timothy 2:15

COACHING

At some level, every student must learn independently of the instructor. Homework, reading, and other assignments must be done without you. To succeed, the student must learn how to learn. A coach must train athletes to do their best work in the one place the coach can't go—on the field. So you must train your students to learn in your absence. You will have direct supervision for only a year or so, but they will need skills that will last a lifetime.

Teach them discipline and organization so they can complete assignments. When you expect the best, more than likely you will receive their best efforts. When you make excuses and rationalize their failures, students will learn to excuse their behavior. A coach doesn't succeed by making excuses for his or her players. Rather, a coach succeeds by expecting their best efforts. Those disciplines last long after the lights on the playing field have been diminished. They are learned behaviors that manifest themselves in other areas of life as well.

Coach good study habits. Your students will become champions.

Avoid using clichés.

"You were born an original.
Don't die a copy."

—Robert Schuller

CLARITY

When you have something to say, make it crisp and clear. You are not only a teacher; you are a communicator. How you say something will directly effect the impact of what you have to say. Good communicators usually have their own checklists. They rehearse their presentations to weed out the words and phrases that impede the transference of ideas.

Avoid vague statements, generalities, and clichés. Stay clear of overly used pop words. Every generation has words or phrases that characterize it. Crossing that "language timeline" could very well bring your communication efforts to a screeching halt. Choose words that mean something to today's culture. A 70s or 80s language is about as useful in reaching today's "millenials" as a flannel graph.

If it's been said a million times, don't say it again. Get rid of tired adjectives. Use superlatives sparingly. Very few things are "the best," "the worst," or "super." Almost nothing is "awesome."

Say what you mean. Say it simply and directly. That will keep your speech from being, well, "old hat."

Keep excellent records.

"It takes less time to do a thing
right than it does to explain
why you did it wrong."

—Henry Wadsworth Longfellow

METHODOLOGY

Don't do your work twice. When you're looking for Information that has already passed through your hands, you're wasting time. Paper trails, computer files, journaling—they all have their place. Too much, and it's mere clutter. Just enough, and it's clear: record keeping is a teaching method. And learning how to record where you've been will give you a better sense of where you are going.

Perhaps it may be said that a good filing system is at the beginning of good teaching habits. For example, a file of old lesson plans can be recycled and used to teach fresh truths. Clippings are the source of great stories that will bring a mundane story to majestic life. Both would be lost without a good storage process.

Record the results of methods you've tried. The what, where, when, and how of your records are signposts that will help you in avoiding repetition and in keeping your presentations up-to-date. No need to reinvent the wheel. Develop a system of record keeping. You'll save hours of time and days of aggravation.

Decorate your classroom walls.

"Decorated walls make the
classroom come alive."

—Linda Toler

ATMOSPHERE

Color communicates. So do shapes and forms. Creativity in your students begins with you—it's "caught" as well as "taught." Your classroom walls can be used as an interesting canvas where the beauty and significance of images may very well spark the artistry of your students. Use your teaching space at every level.

Teach illustration by illustrating.

Model art appreciation with artistic displays.

Let posters reinforce your maxims.

Use colors and images to set the mood for your students.

Rotate bulletin boards to keep them fresh.

Display photos of current events.

Make every inch of space in your classroom work for you and for your students. By creating an imaginative environment, you won't have to work as hard to pry imagination from the sleepy or sullen minds of your students.

Think about lighting. Is there enough? Can it be used to create atmosphere? Look around your classroom. Would you want to study there? If not, maybe it needs a renovation. You might not be authorized to move a wall, but you could seek permission to paint one.

Those little touches might make a big difference.

Build bridges to your students' hearts.

"When God measures a person, He puts a tape around their heart, not their head."

—Lon Woodrum

COMPASSION

The old saying is true: People don't care how much you know until they know how much you care. It's an adage that gives the businessperson a great advantage. It's an even greater advantage for the teacher. For several hours every day, you are the substitute mother, father, sister, or brother for your students. During the school day, they can't be with their families, but they can be with you. Their families' support is in the abstract; yours is concrete.

Your students aren't looking for an expert. They want a mentor: someone who's been where they're going, who understands what they need, who can show them the way. They need friendship as much as philosophy. They need an outstretched hand more than an outmoded fact of history.

There you are—a friendly face in an otherwise morning of madness; a welcomed word after a harrowing journey between the school bus and the schoolroom; a positive reinforcement in a day that otherwise was frustrating.

Be a bridge rather than a wall. Reach out. Reach over. Welcome a new friend. Touch your students' hearts, and you will win their minds.

Emphasize understanding over memorization.

"A well-trained memory is one that permits you to forget everything that isn't worth remembering."

—Battista

COMPREHENSION

Teaching facts is easy. You can train a parrot to repeat information, but it's more difficult to get it to apply that information to its birdcage life. Teaching is more than tossing facts into the classroom atmosphere like cut flowers. It is more like planting a garden. It involves careful preparation, faithful sowing, tender watering, and a determination to keep the weeds of error from interfering with growth.

The goal of teaching is understanding, not mere knowledge. Students haven't really learned until they are able to translate your truths into daily living. Math is more than numbers; it is a problem-solving tool that your students may use to build a career. Computer skills go beyond terms and technologies. Real skill is learning how to use that instrument for individual or corporate blessing.

Teach until the lights go on—until vague principles become vital paths where wondering minds will begin a glorious journey. Comprehension is more important than memorization. Until a student learns to apply facts to faith, the learning cycle is not complete.

Always show students what to do with what they know.

Balance work with play.

"I never did a day's work
in my life. It was all fun."

—Thomas Edison

RECREATION

Learning is hard work. It may be exciting, but it's also difficult. On most school days, students rise too early, eat too little, and earn even less for their efforts. Most aren't at school because it was their chosen activity of the day. The law requires it. No wonder they often look offended when the roll is taken! They know that for the next several hours much will be given to them and much will be required. They will be expected to assimilate in mere minutes the concepts that have taken you years to understand. So give them a break—literally. Hit the "pause" button once in a while.

Give your students a "timely time-out." It will be good for their bodies, minds, and spirits. Set the borders, and then turn them loose for a little playtime. The books will always be there, but the moment is fleeting. In fact, that moment may be the most opportune teaching time. Weave your subject matter into games and downtime activities.

The change will benefit the teacher as much as the student!

Balance justice with mercy.

"He has showed you, O man, what is good. And what does the Lord require of you? To act justly and to love mercy and to walk humbly with your God."

—Micah 6:8

FAIRNESS

A teacher wears many hats: mentor, friend, expert, and even judge. But some students will need mercy more than justice. They'll bring a world of heartache into the classroom with them, and they'll need compassion. They'll need a friend more than they will need a critic, an extended hand rather than a raised voice. Experience will tell you the difference.

But let's face it, others will need a little justice. They'll need to learn that life has a few borders, that responsibility isn't just a spelling word. They'll need to learn respect, discipline, and dependability. Both love and justice are needed, but they must be dealt in equal measure. A "fairness doctrine" isn't just a historical principle, it is a necessity. They see the extremes—too much mercy and too much justice—on an almost daily basis. Criminals walk while victims weep. The accused is judged without benefit of a hearing. Let them see a little balance.

Know when to give a pat on the back and when to hold feet to the fire.

Balance facts with fantasy.

"Facts mean nothing
unless they are rightly
understood, rightly related,
and rightly interpreted."

—R. L. Long

Stan Toler

DREAMING

A wandering mind is a terrible thing to waste. Some of the great inventions and achievements owe their beginnings to a dream. One day a mind wandered—fantasizing about a better society, a better method, or a better application—and Voila! A cure was conceived.

Most learning activities are tedious. Rote memory drills, skill practice, review—a student can tolerate these only in limited doses. Find ways to inject some fantasy time into the day's routine. Of course, those times should be guided and guarded. But rotating both active and passive activities can be beneficial. Alternate the hard work with the fun stuff. Give your students time to do some serious dreaming. Let them fantasize about a better world—and their part in making it that way.

Obviously, daydreaming is as much of a routine as whispers and passed notes. Why not harness it? Give your students creative time—time to let their minds wander past the fences of "what is" to discover "what can be."

Balance the fact-finding with fantasy times by encouraging learners to be dreamers as well.

95

Simplify!
Simplify!
Simplify!

"We must simplify,
simplify, simplify."

—Henry David Thoreau

SIMPLICITY

The most difficult part of the communication process is in making it look easy. Effective communicators work diligently to tear down the fences of misunderstanding. They speak to be understood, not to make an impression. Break out the big words, complex facts, and vague theories, and your audience will soon catch each other's yawns like a cold in kindergarten. Simplify your communication, and even the complex can be comprehended. Simplicity is the key to effective communication.

Examine your presentation carefully. Is the language clear? Are you using too many words? Does it have communication "bridges"? As a matter of fact, every idea can be reduced to a single sentence. Try it. If you can't put your thought into one simple sentence, your audience will not understand your point. Refine your presentation. Break complex ideas into component parts. Reduce every principle to its most basic level, wrap it with a practical illustration, and then present it lovingly to your audience. They will more than appreciate the gift.

Here's a good principle: If the youngest person in your audience can understand what you are saying, everyone will.

Teach the advantages of authority.

"Example is not the main thing in influencing others. It is the only thing."

—Albert Schweitzer

RESPECT

Learning is rare when there is an absence of respect. A teacher who tolerates tardiness, disruptive behavior, foul language, or unruliness harms the student exhibiting these behaviors as well as the entire class. Respect for authority is what levels the field in a classroom. It allows everyone to participate equally.

"Straighten up, or I'll turn you over to the authorities." We've heard it all of our lives. But when you think about it, authority isn't a negative word. Authority suggests that someone is in charge, and that provides a sense of safety. Authority means that someone has the final word, and that provides an atmosphere of responsibility.

Teach your students the positive side of authority, and they will be blessed. Let them live their lives without respecting authority, and they will be cursed. It's too bad that respect for authority can't be given intravenously. But we know that forced reaction causes rebellion. And just like rebellion, respect is catching. When one or more students practice it, it influences the rest. And when the teacher models it, the students take notice.

"Read" and "lead" students.

"Success has many fathers, but failure is always an orphan."

—John F. Kennedy

EVALUATION

Evaluating a student goes beyond the report card. The report card measures only what a student has done. You must evaluate where the student is and where he can go.

Learn to read your students. What are they working on today? Oh, that doesn't mean what their classroom assignment is. What are they working on inside their minds? Their hearts?

What is their main concern? Of course, for the most part, that is the $64,000 question. If you were a mind reader, you probably wouldn't be in the teaching profession. You might be concentrating on the lottery!

But in one sense, you are a mind reader. Your daily interaction with your students has given you great insights into what motivates them—and what completely turns them off. Over time, you learn to read their faces.

Once you can read them, you must then lead them. Where do they need to grow? Where do you want them to go? How will you utilize the knowledge you have gained by reading their countenances and behavior?

Evaluation leads to motivation.

Create an atmosphere of openness.

"Freedom is not the right to do as a person pleases, but the liberty to do as he ought."

—Cicero

FREEDOM

Often, freedom of expression is a constitutional right, except in the classroom. One of the earliest expressions a kindergartner hears is "Shh!" A hundred times a day, the child is told to be quiet—and then first grade comes along. Now the child is constantly asked to speak up. No wonder there's a bit of confusion.

Where's the balance between openness and anarchy? Let your students know that their opinions are valued. Your words of encouragement, your facial expressions, and your gestures are ways to express, "I value what you have to say."

Students also need the opportunity to state their opinions out loud. The teacher often approaches the class session thinking about what he or she will say and teach. An atmosphere of openness in the classroom allows for times when the teacher simply listens.

Let your students know that they don't have to be afraid of giving wrong answers. Let's face it, school days won't be the only time in their lives when they'll give wrong answers. They'll be wrong sometimes as employees, as spouses, or as parents. They might as well get used to taking the risk now.

Teach good sportsmanship.

"It takes a good person to win without boasting and lose without murmuring."

—Johnny Stubbs

FAIR PLAY

That athlete's obnoxious behavior caught live or on tape had its earliest beginning. And often that behavior was born in the classrooms or on the playgrounds of the school where you teach. From the earliest competition on the field or in front of the class, that spoiled-brat behavior was reinforced—sometimes by loud applause and at other times by silent approval.

Each person is unique—just like everybody else! The crowd is comprised of persons, each with a unique personality, unique strengths, and unique weaknesses. And often the rowdy behavior of one is a cry to be seen in the crowd.

Even calling students by their names is important to their sense of recognition. All of us like to hear our name mentioned out loud—no matter how difficult it is to pronounce.

Teaching your students to recognize the individuality of others is a step toward good sportsmanship. Teaching them to make allowances for the strengths and weakness of others is an even greater step.

Training your students to give and take today will help to prevent them from being mere takers tomorrow.

Live by the golden rule.

"The Golden Rule is still the only rule."

—Stan Toler

KINDNESS

Do unto others before they do unto you"
seems to be the norm these days. But
that's not how it should be. Treating people the
way you would like to be treated is not only
socially prudent, it's also professionally
prudent. You are known not only by the
company you keep, but also by the way you
keep your company.

Kindness is, first, an attitude. It seeks the
personal welfare of others above one's own
welfare. It not only recognizes the personal
worth of others; it seeks to make them feel
worthy. How you treat another person begins in
your mind; it begins with how you feel about
that person. For example, a judgmental
attitude will result in judgmental behavior.

Of course, kindness is also an action. The
Scriptures teach us that our deeds express our
devotion. A note, a birthday or anniversary
card, a small gift in honor of an achievement—
these are the tangible expressions of our
concern for others and the things we would
welcome ourselves.

Network with a mentor.

"I use not only my own brains but also all I can borrow."

—Woodrow Wilson

SUPPORT

We really do need each other, and not just because we need companionship. We also need the wisdom and skills of others. The classroom is just the beginning. The knowledge you gained in your professional training doesn't necessarily make you a professional. It will take more. It will take the educated input of your colleagues.

Garnering the experience of others begins with a mentoring relationship. Find someone who is knowledgeable in your area, and then commit to learning from that person. You've been taught that you are personally equipped, and you probably are. But you are still a learner. In fact, you can't be an effective teacher without being an accomplished learner.

Mentoring is a good way to fill in the personal and professional gaps. A more experienced teacher will be the source of a wealth of information that you can utilize in your teaching. A simple cup of coffee may be one of the wisest investments you will ever make. In that informal time together, you may reap the benefits of years of experience — experience that you can't learn from a textbook.

Team up and triumph.

Attend conferences and seminars.

"Learning is a treasure
that accompanies its
owner everywhere."

—Chinese Proverb

LEARNING

Just as teaching is a lifelong commitment, so is learning. "You're never too old to learn" the maxim says. You're never too young either. The patterns you establish at the beginning of your career are the ones that will sustain you throughout it. Learning is a lifelong devotion. You don't learn once—once is not enough. You keep on learning. You take advantage of every opportunity to increase your knowledge and your skills.

Conferences and seminars offer such an opportunity. For a few dollars, usually reimbursed by your school corporation, you can tap into the wellspring of great professional wisdom. At the same time, you can network with other professionals and learn from them.

Conferences and seminars offer not only an opportunity for learning; they offer an opportunity for living. You need a life outside the classroom—a break from the routine. Attending a learning session may be just what the doctor ordered to take your mind off the stress of trying to teach others.

Go ahead and go. Live a little. Learn a lot.

Model good manners.

"Life is so short, but there
is always time enough
for courtesy."

—Ralph Waldo Emerson

COURTESY

The classic expression, "Children have more need of models than critics," is as good for the classroom as it is for the home. "Show and tell" isn't just a school activity; it's a wonderful way to balance profession and expression. What you profess to know is expressed best by what you model. You can't effectively teach your students what you have not learned. Oh, you may be thrown into a substitute-teaching situation—asked to teach a subject that is unfamiliar to you. And you may arrive with a stack of textbooks. But it won't take long for inexperience to surface—usually spotted first by the students in row one. You soon realize that you are more comfortable teaching something in your area of expertise.

Courtesy isn't learned from a textbook; it's learned by seeing courtesy in action. More than likely, the way you treat your students is the way they will treat others. Often, you have more hours to spend with them then their own parents do!

Courtesy is "caught," and you are a carrier.

Maintain a daily teaching journal.

"Journaling is the key to staying fresh in the classroom."

—David Case

JOURNALING

They're everywhere. From card shops to outlet malls, you'll find an abundance of personal journals. Decorated lively or sedately, they have become increasingly popular to people who want to keep a record of their thoughts. Journaling is also popular on the Internet. Personal Web sites offer a place for people to express their personal journeys in HTML. And the number of visits to those sites indicates the real interest people have in observing those journeys.

Journaling is also good for the teacher. It gives him or her a record of methods, as well as an outlet for personal concerns. Lesson plans, illustrations, and audiovisuals can be tracked for future reference. It's also a good way to avoid repetition and to keep the lesson presentation focused and on track.

Journaling also offers the teacher a record of his or her personal progress. Added comments, a thought for the day, a Bible verse—these are interesting signposts that not only give guidance for the immediate but can also be a great source of refreshment and encouragement in the future.

Monitor the progress of former students.

"Never underestimate
the power of a note."

—Norman Vincent Peale

FOLLOW-UP

I wonder what ever became of what's-his-name? Suddenly that thought reminds you of the investment you made in the life of another, and you wonder how that investment has paid off. Teaching isn't like working on a factory line, where nuts and bolts are fused and electrical panels are placed in refrigerators. Teaching is personal. For a few moments in time, people's lives interact in a redeeming or a rugged way.

Naturally you will be curious about the impact accomplished by that interaction. The teacher has an advantage over other professionals. Often, the students in your classroom are siblings—or children of a previous student. If you teach long enough, you will be teaching one to three generations from the same family. Inquire about the others.

Read the newspaper. Some of those leaders whose comments are recorded may have learned their leadership at your hand. And some of those notorious members of your community may have learned their art of rebellion by trying your patience in your classroom!

Send them a note. Affirm them. Let a former student know that your interest didn't die on graduation day.

Further your education.

"It is on the sound education
of the people that the
security and destiny of
every nation chiefly rests."

—Louis Kossuth

SELF-IMPROVEMENT

You get your degree by degrees. The learning journey doesn't end with a walk across a platform. That's only the beginning. That sheepskin is more than a reward; it's a road map. You have just learned how to learn. And the same commitment that resulted in that degree on the wall will need to be renewed from time to time.

You expect your students to further their education, so why not make that personal commitment yourself? Self-improvement is the best home improvement. It helps your self-esteem, and, as a result, you build better relationships with others.

Furthering your education also increases your teaching skills. The knowledge you gain can be duplicated in the life of your students. Every theory, every fact, every discovery can be passed along like a baton in a relay race. The end accomplishments of your students are the by-products of your own education. By improving yourself, you are ultimately improving others. That's what teaching is all about.

Sign up for a class. Join a study group. Be a library regular. Freshen your mind, and you will freshen your teaching.

Read books that strengthen you professionally.

"When a subject becomes totally obsolete, we make it a required course."

—Peter Drucker

INTELLECT

READERS ARE LEADERS" the ad slogan reads, and it's true. Reading puts you a step ahead of the nonreader. Readers know what in the world is going on. They have a grasp of current affairs that nonreaders just don't have. Readers know what people are thinking. No, they're not mind readers; they've just plugged in to the current thought of society. Readers have an edge on the latest in motivational and human potential theories. They are better equipped to lead others. The list goes on and on; readers really are leaders.

Teachers who read are also a step ahead. Education is constantly evolving, and staying current is essential to strengthening your professional skills.

But more than that, reading is essential to intellectual development. With so much emphasis on physical fitness, the development of the mind is often overlooked. Fitness gurus emphasize weight training, aerobics, and proper diet for the health of the body. What about the mind? Do you have a mind-strengthening routine? Mental exercises? A proper mental diet? Do you read junk books or healthy books?

Start an intellectual fitness routine.

Focus on relationships rather than rules.

"It's not how much you do, but how much love you put into what you do that counts."

—Mother Teresa

Stan Toler

FLEXIBILITY

The only exercise some folks get is bending rules. Others are so rigid they probably stand up when they sleep! Rigidity usually limits relationships, because relationships thrive on give and take.

There is a place for rules. The drive to work would be dangerous without them. A tennis game without rules would be more like batting practice. Tennis rules make the game more enjoyable. But the same game would be a nightmare if one of the players contested every shot and demanded a constant reference to the rule book.

If you let them, rules will rule your life. You will be a slave to every jot and tittle, dotting every "i" and crossing every "t." That behavior limits the time you have to invest in relationships. Relationships demand spontaneity. They call for changing plans to include a lunch date, canceling an appointment to run an errand, or skipping a favorite television program to make a phone call. Relationships are "other" focused. They put the needs and welfare of others ahead of personal needs and personal welfare.

Challenge mediocrity.

"Reading is to the mind what exercise is to the body."

—Joseph Addison

DRIVE

Some folks are driven to excel, while others can't seem to get out of "park." Mediocrity is a dangerous malady that causes people to always settle for second best. For the most part, it is a personal choice. Mediocrity begins in the mind. It's like a weed that winds itself around personal ambition and chokes it. If left to grow, it will prevent any personal growth. It even has its own language: "I can't." "I was never able to." "I just don't have what it takes."

Mediocrity must be challenged like an aggressive enemy. Challenge it with education. Books, tapes, Internet sites, and seminars are like swords that can be wielded against the crippling effects of mediocrity.

Challenge it with adventure. Try a new hobby. Plan a trip. Join an interest group. Step out of the box into a brave new world. You'll not only discover new interests and make new friends; you'll fight the enemy of apathy at the same time.

Put your life in "drive," and you'll get a lot farther down the road.

Reward
creativity.

"The greatest use of a life
is to spend it for something
that outlasts it."

—William James

CREATIVITY

Some of the most creative students in your classroom are often some of the most silent. Creativity is like an underground stream. It must be tapped. But once it is discovered, it is a constant source of refreshment. Your job is to make the discovery—to tap the stream of creative talent and bring it to the surface.

First, you must find it. Giving opportunity for creative efforts is a place to start. Class projects, personal assignments, group activity—these are the tools of investigation that could reveal the hidden talents in your classroom.

Then you must reward it. Creative people are usually insecure about their abilities. They need constant affirmation. A word, a note, or public recognition can be the spark that ignites the fire of creativity in that silent student.

Like a coach watching players on the field, you look for the standout. And then you make a personal effort to work with his or her natural talent until it graduates into excellence. With a little bit of attention, that silent student may make the loudest impression.

Rise above pettiness.

"A sign of maturity is when
you go from a thick skin and
a hard heart to a tough skin
and a soft heart."

—Chuck Swindoll

MATURITY

You might as well admit it: some things really bug you! Often, it's not the major problems that stunt your personal growth; it's the minors. It's the little things that get under your skin like a splinter of wood. That tiny fragment can cause not only pain; if left untreated it can cause severe infection.

Maturity is learning to deal with the splinters. It means rising above the things that bring you down, like the petty things that often have names and faces—that faculty policy, the loudmouthed colleague, too few office supplies. the principal that seemingly doesn't notice your efforts.

Sometimes the petty things can be pretty significant. They hinder your progress. They keep you stressed out. They prevent meaningful relationships with other colleagues. It's time to rise above them.

Choose your battles. Some things just aren't worth the cost of your time and energies. If it doesn't fit into your overall plan, then file it in the bottom drawer and refuse to open it. Commit to adjusting for the sake of the cause.

Petty isn't pretty!

Document problems with difficult students.

"Until you do little details carefully, you will never do the big things correctly."

—Zig Ziglar

CAUTION

In days of yore, a man's word was as good as a contract. Parcels of land were bought and sold with nothing but a handshake to seal the deal. Then came the age of litigation. Prenuptial agreements became as sacred as wedding certificates. Coffee cups had to be printed with words of warning about the temperature of their contents. And a three-piece suit could refer to the stages of a court proceeding rather than an article of clothing.

It's a new world for teachers as well. Parent-teacher conferences may now include legal threats, along with inquiries about the curricula. Little Johnny or Jane has the business card of his or her parents' lawyer in the government-approved backpack that has been declared hazardous to childrens' health by a consumer protection group.

Dealing with the bad behavior of the student has also changed. The paddle once used by the principal hangs on the wall of the local museum, and educators must use caution when dealing with bad behavior.

In real estate, the word is "Location, Location, Location!" In education, the word is "Documentation, Documentation, Documentation!"

Establish a daily devotional life.

"May the words of my mouth
and the meditation of my heart
be pleasing in your sight,
O LORD, my Rock and
my Redeemer."

—Psalm 19:14

SPIRITUALITY

The saying goes, "As long as there are tests there will be prayer in school." As a philosopher suggested, there is a God-shaped vacuum inside everyone. We are multidimensional—mental, physical, social, and spiritual beings. To deny the spiritual is to deny a vital part of who we are.

The best thing you can do for yourself, and for your students, is to establish a daily routine of spiritual communion with God. Prayer, Bible reading, and the reading of a devotional book may very well be the most important preparation you will ever make on any given school day.

Talking with God about your day will give you a sense of peace and affirmation. Letting God talk to you through His Word, the Bible, is receiving instruction on an extraordinary level. And devotional writers put your spiritual thoughts into practical words and phrases, not only speaking to you but also speaking for you in expressing your faith in the Almighty.

When you start the day on your knees, you will walk with confidence.

Follow your life's mission.

"There is no poverty that can overtake diligence."

—Japanese Proverb

Stan Toler

PURPOSE

You're not behind that lectern by chance. You're there by choice. It's not just a job; it's a mission. Sometimes it seems like "Mission Impossible," but it is a mission nevertheless. And there is great comfort in knowing that you are fulfilling your purpose. You felt the call of education. You prepared yourself. You sought the right place to practice your skills. Now, here you are!

It's good to know that when the days are long, the air conditioner has broken down, and the community is voting on the local bond issue, you still have a purpose. You are someone significant in the total process. You know who you are and why you are here. Come to think of it, who and why are two of the more important questions in life. When you've answered those questions, you're a couple of blocks ahead of anyone else in the human race.

Focus on your mission. Don't be sidetracked by finances, politics, or societal changes. You are called to transfer classic truths to contemporary minds.

Encourage compassion among students.

"If you want others to be happy, practice compassion."

—Edward Hayes

BROTHERHOOD

Reality shows have captured the television audience. "Caught on tape" is the new ambulance chase. Now you can ride with the police as they pursue fleeing criminals. "Who's going to be voted off the island?" is the water-cooler question of the day. Web cameras have opened the blinds of society until almost nothing is hidden.

But the technology that was supposed to bring us together has actually driven us apart. Now we are the generation of the suspicious. Too many trusted servants have been caught with their hands in the proverbial cookie jar. We now have to work hard at putting our faith in another.

That mistrust has invaded the classroom as well. The teacher is not only called to teach facts and philosophies, but also a sense of community. "No man is an island" is still the thought for the day. No matter what race, gender, or origin we are, we all are a part of one another.

Compassion ought to be inserted into the lesson plan. Getting along is just as important as getting ahead.

Meet life's challenges one day at a time.

"There is no thrill quite
like doing something you
didn't know you could."

—Marjorie Holmes

SERENITY

Life isn't so bad when you live it in chunks of time. None of us would want to live it all at once. No matter what the television psychics say, we really don't want to know what the future holds. For some, it would be far too painful to see around the bend.

The Scripture advises us not to borrow on tomorrow's troubles. Live for today and hope for tomorrow. That's great advice for those who long for a little peace of mind in the turmoil of these times.

Serenity is a decision—a decision of trust. It is a decision to rest your mind and spirit in the timeless promises of a God who promised His care and keeping—a decision to surrender your past to His forgiveness and your future to His grace.

At your retirement, when you reflect on the challenges you have faced in your career, you will wonder how you ever survived. But you probably will survive, not because of your superior skills but because of your faith.

Take the challenge—one day at a time.

Trust God's Word as the standard for morality.

"Teach me, O LORD, to follow
your decrees; then I will
keep them to the end."

—Psalm 119:33

SCRIPTURE

Everything is relative," some modern philosophers suggest. But the problem is, there are times when you need absolute answers for real-life situations. That's an "Aha!" moment! God's Word, the Bible, is just such a source. This God-inspired book is the best-selling book of all time. Why? Because it can be trusted—absolutely! Every printing contains the same principles. The Scriptures form the spiritual grid for living life to the fullest.

Life's little surprises are no surprise when your frame of reference is the Bible. Its history is as accurate as its prophecy. It spans millenniums with a message of forgiveness and hope. It helps us understand human behavior and divine intervention.

If there is no last word on a standard of conduct, then chaos is king. But the Scriptures are God's final answer. They provide the insights necessary for order and civility. Read them with confidence. Apply their truths with the assurance that they will make a difference in your life and in the lives of those for whom you are responsible.

Read the Bible and reap.

Connect actions with consequences.

"After the fire, ashes;
after the rain, roses."

—Moroccan Proverb

RESPONSIBILITY

I t's a fact of life: For every action there is a reaction. Our words and deeds have a lasting influence, like ripples on the pond when a pebble is tossed in. And taking responsibility for those ripples is part of the maturing process.

Teaching young people to be responsible for their behavior is as vital as teaching them geometry. In fact, it will probably be of greater significance. In their higher education, careers, relationships, and homes, understanding the connection between actions and consequences is absolutely necessary to making good adjustments.

Responsibility is learned early in the classroom experience. Failure to study for the test, a missed assignment deadline, tardiness— these are life lessons for the student. And students must know that a consequence follows their action (or inaction).

Make allowance for poor performance, and you have done a great disservice to your students. Allow them to give an account for their actions, and you have given them a helpful nudge out of the nest into the real world.

Relax in faith.

"There is no conceivable
situation in which it is
not safe to trust God."

—J. Oswald Sanders

TRUST

Faith is simple. Each morning you gather your books, the papers you graded the night before, and perhaps a lunch. Placing them in the car, you begin looking for the car keys. Once they're found, you get in the driver's seat, put a key into the ignition, and turn it. The engine starts, and you're on your way to another exciting school day. Faith was displayed in the whole process. From your belief that your job was waiting for you, to the belief the car would start once you turned the ignition key, you were trusting in the power and provision of another.

You didn't have to fully understand any of it to enjoy its benefits. You simply trusted. Spiritual faith is just like that. You don't have to understand the whole process of forgiveness, peace of mind, daily supply, or hope in Heaven; you simply trust the power and provision of God.

Relax. He won't fail you. Because God is eternal, He's already visited this day. He knew every hour of it before the first stars were born.

Pray for your students by name.

"A lot of kneeling keeps
us in good standing."

—Jim Marshall

PRAYER

Name-dropper" isn't a negative conno-
tation when it comes to mentioning
your students' names in prayer. You have the
awesome opportunity to take their individual
concerns to the God of the universe. You don't
have to make a loud declaration about it—or
any declaration at all. You can just simply do it.
You can act as your students' ambassador
before the throne of Heaven.

When you think about it, it may be one of
the most important things you can do for
yourself and for your students. Each of you has
spiritual, emotional, or relational needs that
are known only to that person. On a daily
basis, you can petition God to meet those needs
out of His loving kindness and merciful supply.

Policy may prohibit you from even mentioning it, but policies can't stop prayer. It can
happen even in the classroom—in times of
silent prayer. Whether you pray for your
students in your private devotional time or
silently in person, you can be assured that
prayer changes things.

Find a prayer partner.

"Fervent, believing prayer
lies at the root of all
personal godliness."

—William Carey

CAMARADERIE

There really is strength in numbers. Especially when it comes to prayer. The Bible says that when two agree on earth concerning a matter, it will gain the attention of Heaven.

Camaraderie among faculty members is truly a powerful force. It can bind persons together in a common purpose, emanate healing to those who are hurt, and provide a resource for facing the stress of everyday teaching.

But when people of faith meet together, they have an even greater resource. A third party is involved: God. And even as they join hands together before Him, they join hearts. Their common devotion gives them a sense of community, even in a secular setting.

Find a prayer partner. In this politically correct age, the meeting time often must be discreet, but it can be arranged. Turn that lunchtime into a "power lunch." Make an appointment and bring yourselves, your students, your faculty, and your school system before the eternal God. Who knows? You may not only find a prayer partner; you may make a new best friend.

Never forget the language of love.

"I not only want to be loved, I want to be told that I'm loved."

—George Elliot

LOVE

You probably know about the Romance languages, but do you know about the language of love? It is, at once, the gentlest and the most powerful language ever uttered. The language contains such words as patient, kind, long-suffering, humble, polite, forgiving, honest.

Obviously, this isn't a language that can be learned from a correspondence course, a software program, or a night class. It is born of personal faith and is a language that is best spoken by one whose heart is at peace with God.

Even in a multicultural society, it is a language understood by all. Often it doesn't even require words to be expressed. It simply speaks with acts of consideration, selfless behavior, compassion, and understanding. It crosses lines of color with brotherhood, and it crosses economic lines with community.

It is the language of a peaceful classroom as well. Led by the teacher, the language of love breaks down the barriers that separate students from other students and students from faculty.

Make sure you are fluent in the language of love.

Work with parents to raise a child.

"We never know the love of
a parent until we become
parents ourselves."

—Henry Ward Beecher

PARTNERSHIP

It takes a team to raise a child. Though the pressure is on the starting lineup—the parents—it takes a pretty good bench—the teachers—to round out the team. Teachers offer the strength of their skills and their emotional support to the parental team. Their contribution to the game is highly significant. Considering they have more playing time than the parental team during the average weekday, their actions contribute to the wins and the losses in no small way.

The strength of a winning team is in its bench. Without the support of the equally trained support players, the overall team just wouldn't be complete. Parents and teachers are the team, and they have an important partnership. As they support each other by their words or actions, students often watch them very closely and play off their relationships.

Teachers are well advised to remember that they are not THE TEAM. They are a part of the team. Their best efforts are enhanced when they work as partners with the parental team.

Let your walk match your talk.

"Integrity is the integration of one's life around core values."

—William Lawrence

EXAMPLE

You've heard the expression, "Seeing is believing." That is true of teaching as well. Teachers are paid to talk—every day, for almost the entire day. Much of what they say is heard, and some of what they say is tuned out. Often the "tune out" is the result of a lack of credibility. When the teacher's position is "Do as I say" rather than "Do as I do," the result is a communication barrier.

The best teachers model the truths they proclaim. They are living examples of the benefits of an education. Telling students they ought to further their education is one thing; showing them the positive character and personality of a lifelong learner is another. It's too bad there isn't a college course called Example 101, because a passing grade in that course would give you a great teaching advantage.

Students who have seen kindness exemplified in front of the classroom, for example, best receive lectures on kindness. Brotherhood is an abstract principle until it is modeled by a teacher who accepts his or her students as they are.

Combine lectures with living

Finish well!

"If all of this world falls from the truth, I will stand!"

—Athanasius

ENDURANCE

The crowd cheers as the marathon runner staggers across the finish line. The medal of victory is draped around his neck. It's a beautiful scene, and it's too bad that it isn't duplicated on a teacher's retirement day!

Often, the teacher simply empties a desk, shakes a few hands, and silently walks out the door. It ought to be reversed, you know. Teachers ought to get the cheers and the medals, because the same dynamics that bring the runner to the finish line bring the teacher to retirement day.

The runner must have a good start and stay focused on the finish line. Everything else is incidental. To the runner, the goal is the most important thing. This is true for the teacher as well.

The runner must also be willing to pay the price: tired muscles, discouragement, bravery against the elements, competition from other runners.

It's true for the teacher as well.

And finally the runner must finish well. The problems are forgotten, the competitors are congratulated, and the prize is accepted without remorse. It's true for the teacher as well.

About the Author

Stan Toler is senior pastor of Trinity Church of the Nazarene in Oklahoma City, Oklahoma, and hosts the television program "Leadership Today." For the past ten years he has taught seminars for INJOY Group—a leadership development institute. Toler has written over forty books, including his best-sellers God Has Never Failed Me, But He Sure Has Scared Me to Death a Few Times and The Five-Star Church.

To Contact the Author

Stan Toler
P. O. Box 892170
Oklahoma City, OK 73189-2170
E-mail: stoler1107@aol.com
Web site: www.StanToler.net